THE
3-MINUTE

LEADERSHIP

JOURNAL

FOR KIDS

✏ This Awesome Journal Belongs To:

Blank Classic

The 3-Minute Leadership Journal
116 numbered pages - 120 total pages
A5 (5.83 x 8.27)

Design © 2021 Blank Classic

Blank Classic

Mailing address:
Blank Classic
PO BOX 4608
Main Station Terminal
349 West Georgia Street
Vancouver, BC
Canada, V6B 4A1

Cover design by: Lauren Dick
Interior design by: Lauren Dick

ISBN: 978-1-77476-132-8

FIRST EDITION / FIRST PRINTING

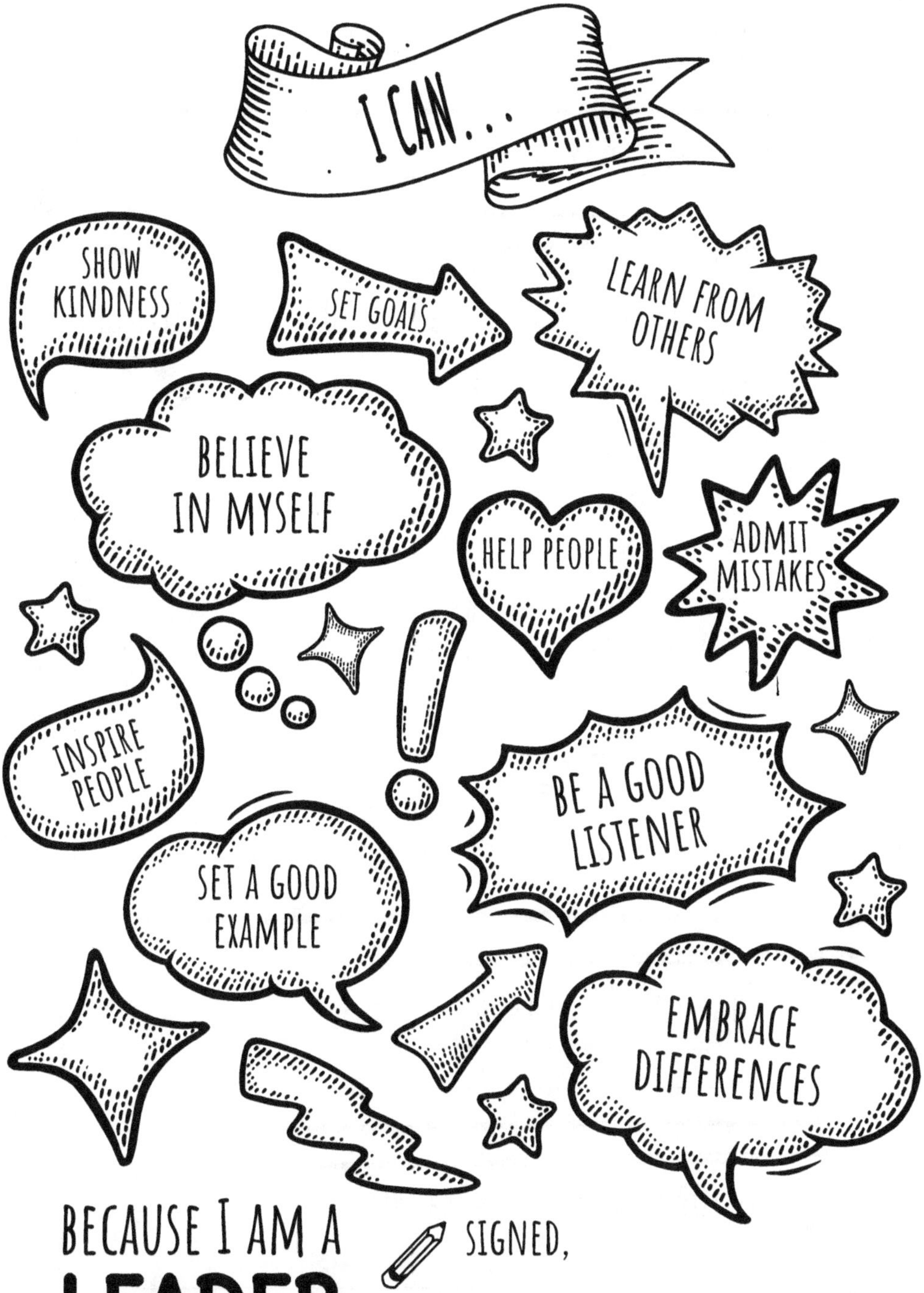

BECAUSE I AM A

LEADER

SIGNED,

____

DATE: S M T W TH F S __ / __ / __

🏆 OVERALL TODAY WAS: ☆ ☆ ☆ ☆ ☆

😄 TODAY'S TRIUMPHS

_____
_____
_____
_____
_____
_____
_____
_____
_____
_____
_____

🤔 TODAY'S CHALLENGES

_____
_____
_____
_____
_____
_____
_____
_____
_____
_____
_____

💡 WHAT I LEARNED FROM TODAY:

_____

🏆 MY TOP GOAL FOR TOMORROW:

_____

1

DRAW ABOUT IT

DATE: S M T W TH F S   __ / __ / __

OVERALL TODAY WAS: ☆ ☆ ☆ ☆ ☆

😀 **TODAY'S TRIUMPHS**

_____
_____
_____
_____
_____
_____
_____
_____
_____
_____

🤔 **TODAY'S CHALLENGES**

_____
_____
_____
_____
_____
_____
_____
_____
_____
_____

💡 **WHAT I LEARNED FROM TODAY:**

_____

🏆 **MY TOP GOAL FOR TOMORROW:**

_____

DRAW ABOUT IT

DATE: S M T W TH F S __ / __ / __

OVERALL TODAY WAS: ☆ ☆ ☆ ☆ ☆

😄 TODAY'S TRIUMPHS

_____
_____
_____
_____
_____
_____
_____
_____
_____
_____

😋 TODAY'S CHALLENGES

_____
_____
_____
_____
_____
_____
_____
_____
_____
_____

💡 WHAT I LEARNED FROM TODAY:

_____

🏆 MY TOP GOAL FOR TOMORROW:

_____

DRAW ABOUT IT

DATE: S M T W TH F S __ / __ / __

OVERALL TODAY WAS: ☆ ☆ ☆ ☆ ☆

😄 TODAY'S TRIUMPHS

_____
_____
_____
_____
_____
_____
_____
_____
_____
_____

🤔 TODAY'S CHALLENGES

_____
_____
_____
_____
_____
_____
_____
_____
_____
_____

💡 WHAT I LEARNED FROM TODAY:

_____

🏆 MY TOP GOAL FOR TOMORROW:

_____

DRAW ABOUT IT

DATE: S M T W TH F S __ / __ / __

📊 OVERALL TODAY WAS: ☆ ☆ ☆ ☆ ☆

😄 TODAY'S TRIUMPHS

_____

_____

_____

_____

_____

_____

_____

_____

_____

🤔 TODAY'S CHALLENGES

_____

_____

_____

_____

_____

_____

_____

_____

_____

💡 WHAT I LEARNED FROM TODAY:

_____

🏆 MY TOP GOAL FOR TOMORROW:

_____

DRAW ABOUT IT

DATE: S M T W TH F S __ / __ / __

OVERALL TODAY WAS: ☆ ☆ ☆ ☆ ☆

☺ TODAY'S TRIUMPHS

_____
_____
_____
_____
_____
_____
_____
_____
_____
_____
_____

😋 TODAY'S CHALLENGES

_____
_____
_____
_____
_____
_____
_____
_____
_____
_____
_____

💡 WHAT I LEARNED FROM TODAY:

_____

🏆 MY TOP GOAL FOR TOMORROW:

_____

DRAW ABOUT IT

DATE: S M T W TH F S __ / __ / __

⛰ OVERALL TODAY WAS: ☆ ☆ ☆ ☆ ☆

😄 TODAY'S TRIUMPHS

_____
_____
_____
_____
_____
_____
_____
_____
_____
_____
_____

🤔 TODAY'S CHALLENGES

_____
_____
_____
_____
_____
_____
_____
_____
_____
_____
_____

💡 WHAT I LEARNED FROM TODAY:

_____

🏆 MY TOP GOAL FOR TOMORROW:

_____

DRAW ABOUT IT

DATE: S M T W TH F S ___ / ___ / ___

OVERALL TODAY WAS: ☆ ☆ ☆ ☆ ☆

😄 TODAY'S TRIUMPHS

_____
_____
_____
_____
_____
_____
_____
_____
_____
_____

🤔 TODAY'S CHALLENGES

_____
_____
_____
_____
_____
_____
_____
_____
_____
_____

💡 WHAT I LEARNED FROM TODAY:

_____

🏆 MY TOP GOAL FOR TOMORROW:

_____

DRAW ABOUT IT

DATE: S M T W TH F S __ / __ / __

OVERALL TODAY WAS: ☆ ☆ ☆ ☆ ☆

☺ TODAY'S TRIUMPHS

_____
_____
_____
_____
_____
_____
_____
_____
_____

😋 TODAY'S CHALLENGES

_____
_____
_____
_____
_____
_____
_____
_____
_____

💡 WHAT I LEARNED FROM TODAY:

_____

🏆 MY TOP GOAL FOR TOMORROW:

_____

DRAW ABOUT IT

DATE: S M T W TH F S __ / __ / __

📊 OVERALL TODAY WAS: ☆ ☆ ☆ ☆ ☆

😄 TODAY'S TRIUMPHS

_____
_____
_____
_____
_____
_____
_____
_____
_____
_____

🤔 TODAY'S CHALLENGES

_____
_____
_____
_____
_____
_____
_____
_____
_____
_____

💡 WHAT I LEARNED FROM TODAY:

_____

🏆 MY TOP GOAL FOR TOMORROW:

_____

DRAW ABOUT IT

DATE: S M T W TH F S __ / __ /__

🏆 OVERALL TODAY WAS: ☆ ☆ ☆ ☆ ☆

😄 TODAY'S TRIUMPHS

_____
_____
_____
_____
_____
_____
_____
_____
_____
_____

🤔 TODAY'S CHALLENGES

_____
_____
_____
_____
_____
_____
_____
_____
_____
_____

💡 WHAT I LEARNED FROM TODAY:

_____

🏆 MY TOP GOAL FOR TOMORROW:

_____

DRAW ABOUT IT

DATE: S M T W TH F S __/__/__

🏆 OVERALL TODAY WAS: ☆ ☆ ☆ ☆ ☆

😄 TODAY'S TRIUMPHS

_____
_____
_____
_____
_____
_____
_____
_____
_____
_____

😋 TODAY'S CHALLENGES

_____
_____
_____
_____
_____
_____
_____
_____
_____
_____

💡 WHAT I LEARNED FROM TODAY:

_____

🏆 MY TOP GOAL FOR TOMORROW:

_____

DRAW ABOUT IT

DATE: S M T W TH F S __ / __ / __

🏆 OVERALL TODAY WAS: ☆ ☆ ☆ ☆ ☆

😄 TODAY'S TRIUMPHS

_____
_____
_____
_____
_____
_____
_____
_____
_____
_____
_____

🫤 TODAY'S CHALLENGES

_____
_____
_____
_____
_____
_____
_____
_____
_____
_____
_____

💡 WHAT I LEARNED FROM TODAY:

_____

🏆 MY TOP GOAL FOR TOMORROW:

_____

DRAW ABOUT IT

DATE: S M T W TH F S __ / __ / __

🏆 OVERALL TODAY WAS: ☆ ☆ ☆ ☆ ☆

😄 TODAY'S TRIUMPHS

_____
_____
_____
_____
_____
_____
_____
_____
_____
_____

😋 TODAY'S CHALLENGES

_____
_____
_____
_____
_____
_____
_____
_____
_____
_____

💡 WHAT I LEARNED FROM TODAY:

_____

🏆 MY TOP GOAL FOR TOMORROW:

_____

DRAW ABOUT IT

DATE: S M T W TH F S __ / __ / __

🏆 OVERALL TODAY WAS: ☆ ☆ ☆ ☆ ☆

😄 TODAY'S TRIUMPHS

_____
_____
_____
_____
_____
_____
_____
_____
_____
_____

😋 TODAY'S CHALLENGES

_____
_____
_____
_____
_____
_____
_____
_____
_____
_____

💡 WHAT I LEARNED FROM TODAY:

_____

🏆 MY TOP GOAL FOR TOMORROW:

_____

DRAW ABOUT IT

DATE: S M T W TH F S ___ / ___ / ___

OVERALL TODAY WAS: ☆ ☆ ☆ ☆ ☆

☺ **TODAY'S TRIUMPHS**

_____

_____

_____

_____

_____

_____

_____

_____

_____

_____

🤔 **TODAY'S CHALLENGES**

_____

_____

_____

_____

_____

_____

_____

_____

_____

💡 **WHAT I LEARNED FROM TODAY:**

_____

🏆 **MY TOP GOAL FOR TOMORROW:**

_____

DRAW ABOUT IT

DATE: S M T W TH F S __ / __ / __

🏆 OVERALL TODAY WAS: ☆ ☆ ☆ ☆ ☆

😄 TODAY'S TRIUMPHS

_____
_____
_____
_____
_____
_____
_____
_____
_____
_____

🤔 TODAY'S CHALLENGES

_____
_____
_____
_____
_____
_____
_____
_____
_____
_____

💡 WHAT I LEARNED FROM TODAY:

_____

🏆 MY TOP GOAL FOR TOMORROW:

_____

DRAW ABOUT IT

DATE: S M T W TH F S __ / __ / __

OVERALL TODAY WAS: ☆ ☆ ☆ ☆ ☆

😄 TODAY'S TRIUMPHS

_____
_____
_____
_____
_____
_____
_____
_____
_____
_____

😋 TODAY'S CHALLENGES

_____
_____
_____
_____
_____
_____
_____
_____
_____
_____

💡 WHAT I LEARNED FROM TODAY:

_____

🏆 MY TOP GOAL FOR TOMORROW:

_____

DRAW ABOUT IT

DATE: S M T W TH F S __ / __ / __

🏆 OVERALL TODAY WAS: ☆ ☆ ☆ ☆ ☆

😄 TODAY'S TRIUMPHS

_____
_____
_____
_____
_____
_____
_____
_____
_____
_____

🤔 TODAY'S CHALLENGES

_____
_____
_____
_____
_____
_____
_____
_____
_____
_____

💡 WHAT I LEARNED FROM TODAY:

_____

🏆 MY TOP GOAL FOR TOMORROW:

_____

DRAW ABOUT IT

DATE: S M T W TH F S   __ / __ / __

📊 OVERALL TODAY WAS: ☆ ☆ ☆ ☆ ☆

😄 TODAY'S TRIUMPHS

_____
_____
_____
_____
_____
_____
_____
_____
_____
_____

🤔 TODAY'S CHALLENGES

_____
_____
_____
_____
_____
_____
_____
_____
_____
_____

💡 WHAT I LEARNED FROM TODAY:

_____

🏆 MY TOP GOAL FOR TOMORROW:

_____

DRAW ABOUT IT

DATE: S M T W TH F S __ / __ / __

🏆 OVERALL TODAY WAS: ☆ ☆ ☆ ☆ ☆

😄 TODAY'S TRIUMPHS

_____
_____
_____
_____
_____
_____
_____
_____
_____
_____
_____

😋 TODAY'S CHALLENGES

_____
_____
_____
_____
_____
_____
_____
_____
_____
_____
_____

💡 WHAT I LEARNED FROM TODAY:

_____

🏆 MY TOP GOAL FOR TOMORROW:

_____

DRAW ABOUT IT

DATE: S M T W TH F S __ / __ / __

OVERALL TODAY WAS: ☆ ☆ ☆ ☆ ☆

😄 TODAY'S TRIUMPHS

_____
_____
_____
_____
_____
_____
_____
_____
_____
_____

🤔 TODAY'S CHALLENGES

_____
_____
_____
_____
_____
_____
_____
_____
_____
_____

💡 WHAT I LEARNED FROM TODAY:

_____

🏆 MY TOP GOAL FOR TOMORROW:

_____

DRAW ABOUT IT

DATE: S M T W TH F S __ / __ / __

⛰️ OVERALL TODAY WAS: ☆ ☆ ☆ ☆ ☆

😄 TODAY'S TRIUMPHS

_____
_____
_____
_____
_____
_____
_____
_____
_____
_____

🤭 TODAY'S CHALLENGES

_____
_____
_____
_____
_____
_____
_____
_____
_____
_____

💡 WHAT I LEARNED FROM TODAY:

_____

🏆 MY TOP GOAL FOR TOMORROW:

_____

DRAW ABOUT IT

DATE: S M T W TH F S __ / __ / __

OVERALL TODAY WAS: ☆ ☆ ☆ ☆ ☆

😄 TODAY'S TRIUMPHS

_____
_____
_____
_____
_____
_____
_____
_____
_____
_____

😋 TODAY'S CHALLENGES

_____
_____
_____
_____
_____
_____
_____
_____
_____
_____

💡 WHAT I LEARNED FROM TODAY:

_____

🏆 MY TOP GOAL FOR TOMORROW:

_____

DRAW ABOUT IT

DATE: S M T W TH F S __ / __ / __

⬛ OVERALL TODAY WAS: ☆ ☆ ☆ ☆ ☆

😄 TODAY'S TRIUMPHS

_____
_____
_____
_____
_____
_____
_____
_____
_____
_____
_____

🤔 TODAY'S CHALLENGES

_____
_____
_____
_____
_____
_____
_____
_____
_____
_____
_____

💡 WHAT I LEARNED FROM TODAY:

_____

🏆 MY TOP GOAL FOR TOMORROW:

_____

DRAW ABOUT IT

DATE: S M T W TH F S __/__/__

OVERALL TODAY WAS: ☆ ☆ ☆ ☆ ☆

😄 TODAY'S TRIUMPHS

_____
_____
_____
_____
_____
_____
_____
_____
_____
_____

🤔 TODAY'S CHALLENGES

_____
_____
_____
_____
_____
_____
_____
_____
_____
_____

💡 WHAT I LEARNED FROM TODAY:

_____

🏆 MY TOP GOAL FOR TOMORROW:

_____

DRAW ABOUT IT

DATE: S M T W TH F S __ / __ / __

OVERALL TODAY WAS: ☆ ☆ ☆ ☆ ☆

😄 TODAY'S TRIUMPHS

_____
_____
_____
_____
_____
_____
_____
_____
_____
_____

🤔 TODAY'S CHALLENGES

_____
_____
_____
_____
_____
_____
_____
_____
_____
_____

💡 WHAT I LEARNED FROM TODAY:

_____

🏆 MY TOP GOAL FOR TOMORROW:

_____

DRAW ABOUT IT

DATE: S M T W TH F S __ / __ / __

🏆 OVERALL TODAY WAS: ☆ ☆ ☆ ☆ ☆

😄 TODAY'S TRIUMPHS

_____
_____
_____
_____
_____
_____
_____
_____
_____
_____

🤔 TODAY'S CHALLENGES

_____
_____
_____
_____
_____
_____
_____
_____
_____
_____

💡 WHAT I LEARNED FROM TODAY:

_____

🏆 MY TOP GOAL FOR TOMORROW:

_____

DRAW ABOUT IT

DATE: S M T W TH F S __ / __ / __

OVERALL TODAY WAS: ☆ ☆ ☆ ☆ ☆

😄 TODAY'S TRIUMPHS

_____
_____
_____
_____
_____
_____
_____
_____
_____
_____

🤭 TODAY'S CHALLENGES

_____
_____
_____
_____
_____
_____
_____
_____
_____
_____

💡 WHAT I LEARNED FROM TODAY:

_____

🏆 MY TOP GOAL FOR TOMORROW:

_____

DRAW ABOUT IT

DATE: S M T W TH F S __ / __ / __

🏆 OVERALL TODAY WAS: ☆ ☆ ☆ ☆ ☆

😄 TODAY'S TRIUMPHS

_____
_____
_____
_____
_____
_____
_____
_____
_____
_____

😛 TODAY'S CHALLENGES

_____
_____
_____
_____
_____
_____
_____
_____
_____
_____

💡 WHAT I LEARNED FROM TODAY:

_____

🏆 MY TOP GOAL FOR TOMORROW:

_____

DRAW ABOUT IT

DATE: S M T W TH F S __ / __ /__

⬜ OVERALL TODAY WAS: ☆ ☆ ☆ ☆ ☆

😄 TODAY'S TRIUMPHS

_____
_____
_____
_____
_____
_____
_____
_____
_____
_____

😋 TODAY'S CHALLENGES

_____
_____
_____
_____
_____
_____
_____
_____
_____
_____

💡 WHAT I LEARNED FROM TODAY:

_____

🏆 MY TOP GOAL FOR TOMORROW:

_____

DRAW ABOUT IT

DATE: S M T W TH F S __ / __ / __

⬛ OVERALL TODAY WAS: ☆ ☆ ☆ ☆ ☆

😄 TODAY'S TRIUMPHS

_____
_____
_____
_____
_____
_____
_____
_____
_____
_____

😋 TODAY'S CHALLENGES

_____
_____
_____
_____
_____
_____
_____
_____
_____
_____

💡 WHAT I LEARNED FROM TODAY:

_____

🏆 MY TOP GOAL FOR TOMORROW:

_____

DRAW ABOUT IT

DATE: S M T W TH F S __ / __ / __

🏆 OVERALL TODAY WAS: ☆ ☆ ☆ ☆ ☆

😄 TODAY'S TRIUMPHS

_____
_____
_____
_____
_____
_____
_____
_____
_____
_____
_____

😋 TODAY'S CHALLENGES

_____
_____
_____
_____
_____
_____
_____
_____
_____
_____
_____

💡 WHAT I LEARNED FROM TODAY:

_____

🏆 MY TOP GOAL FOR TOMORROW:

_____

DRAW ABOUT IT

DATE: S M T W TH F S __ / __ / __

🏆 OVERALL TODAY WAS: ☆ ☆ ☆ ☆ ☆

😄 TODAY'S TRIUMPHS

_____
_____
_____
_____
_____
_____
_____
_____
_____
_____

🤔 TODAY'S CHALLENGES

_____
_____
_____
_____
_____
_____
_____
_____
_____
_____

💡 WHAT I LEARNED FROM TODAY:

_____

🏆 MY TOP GOAL FOR TOMORROW:

_____

DRAW ABOUT IT

DATE: S M T W TH F S __ / __ / __

🏆 OVERALL TODAY WAS: ☆ ☆ ☆ ☆ ☆

😄 TODAY'S TRIUMPHS

_____
_____
_____
_____
_____
_____
_____
_____
_____
_____

🤔 TODAY'S CHALLENGES

_____
_____
_____
_____
_____
_____
_____
_____
_____
_____

💡 WHAT I LEARNED FROM TODAY:

_____

🏆 MY TOP GOAL FOR TOMORROW:

_____

DRAW ABOUT IT

DATE: S M T W TH F S __ / __ / __

🏆 OVERALL TODAY WAS: ☆ ☆ ☆ ☆ ☆

😄 TODAY'S TRIUMPHS

_____
_____
_____
_____
_____
_____
_____
_____
_____
_____

😋 TODAY'S CHALLENGES

_____
_____
_____
_____
_____
_____
_____
_____
_____
_____

💡 WHAT I LEARNED FROM TODAY:

_____

🏆 MY TOP GOAL FOR TOMORROW:

_____

DRAW ABOUT IT

DATE: S M T W TH F S __ / __ / __

OVERALL TODAY WAS: ☆ ☆ ☆ ☆ ☆

😃 TODAY'S TRIUMPHS

_____
_____
_____
_____
_____
_____
_____
_____
_____
_____

🤔 TODAY'S CHALLENGES

_____
_____
_____
_____
_____
_____
_____
_____
_____
_____

💡 WHAT I LEARNED FROM TODAY:

_____

🏆 MY TOP GOAL FOR TOMORROW:

_____

DRAW ABOUT IT

DATE: S M T W TH F S __ / __ / __

🏆 OVERALL TODAY WAS: ☆ ☆ ☆ ☆ ☆

😄 TODAY'S TRIUMPHS

_____
_____
_____
_____
_____
_____
_____
_____
_____
_____

🤤 TODAY'S CHALLENGES

_____
_____
_____
_____
_____
_____
_____
_____
_____
_____

💡 WHAT I LEARNED FROM TODAY:

_____

🏆 MY TOP GOAL FOR TOMORROW:

_____

DRAW ABOUT IT

DATE: S M T W TH F S __ / __ / __

OVERALL TODAY WAS: ☆ ☆ ☆ ☆ ☆

😄 TODAY'S TRIUMPHS

_____
_____
_____
_____
_____
_____
_____
_____
_____
_____

😛 TODAY'S CHALLENGES

_____
_____
_____
_____
_____
_____
_____
_____
_____
_____

💡 WHAT I LEARNED FROM TODAY:

_____

🏆 MY TOP GOAL FOR TOMORROW:

_____

DRAW ABOUT IT

DATE: S M T W TH F S __ / __ /__

🏆 OVERALL TODAY WAS: ☆ ☆ ☆ ☆ ☆

😄 TODAY'S TRIUMPHS

_____
_____
_____
_____
_____
_____
_____
_____
_____
_____

😋 TODAY'S CHALLENGES

_____
_____
_____
_____
_____
_____
_____
_____
_____
_____

💡 WHAT I LEARNED FROM TODAY:

_____

🏆 MY TOP GOAL FOR TOMORROW:

_____

DRAW ABOUT IT

DATE: S M T W TH F S __/__/__

🏆 OVERALL TODAY WAS: ☆ ☆ ☆ ☆ ☆

😄 TODAY'S TRIUMPHS

_____
_____
_____
_____
_____
_____
_____
_____
_____

🤔 TODAY'S CHALLENGES

_____
_____
_____
_____
_____
_____
_____
_____
_____

💡 WHAT I LEARNED FROM TODAY:

_____

🏆 MY TOP GOAL FOR TOMORROW:

_____

DRAW ABOUT IT

DATE: S M T W TH F S __/__/__

OVERALL TODAY WAS: ☆ ☆ ☆ ☆ ☆

😄 **TODAY'S TRIUMPHS**

_____
_____
_____
_____
_____
_____
_____
_____
_____
_____

😋 **TODAY'S CHALLENGES**

_____
_____
_____
_____
_____
_____
_____
_____
_____
_____

💡 **WHAT I LEARNED FROM TODAY:**

_____

🏆 **MY TOP GOAL FOR TOMORROW:**

_____

DRAW ABOUT IT

DATE: S M T W TH F S ___/___/___

OVERALL TODAY WAS: ☆ ☆ ☆ ☆ ☆

☺ TODAY'S TRIUMPHS

_____
_____
_____
_____
_____
_____
_____
_____
_____
_____

🤔 TODAY'S CHALLENGES

_____
_____
_____
_____
_____
_____
_____
_____
_____
_____

💡 WHAT I LEARNED FROM TODAY:

_____

🏆 MY TOP GOAL FOR TOMORROW:

_____

85

DRAW ABOUT IT

DATE: S M T W TH F S __ / __ / __

🏆 OVERALL TODAY WAS: ☆ ☆ ☆ ☆ ☆

😄 TODAY'S TRIUMPHS

_____
_____
_____
_____
_____
_____
_____
_____
_____
_____
_____

🤭 TODAY'S CHALLENGES

_____
_____
_____
_____
_____
_____
_____
_____
_____
_____
_____

💡 WHAT I LEARNED FROM TODAY:

_____

🏆 MY TOP GOAL FOR TOMORROW:

_____

DRAW ABOUT IT

DATE: S M T W TH F S __/__/__

🏆 OVERALL TODAY WAS: ☆ ☆ ☆ ☆ ☆

😄 TODAY'S TRIUMPHS

_____
_____
_____
_____
_____
_____
_____
_____
_____
_____

🤔 TODAY'S CHALLENGES

_____
_____
_____
_____
_____
_____
_____
_____
_____
_____

💡 WHAT I LEARNED FROM TODAY:

_____

🏆 MY TOP GOAL FOR TOMORROW:

_____

DRAW ABOUT IT

DATE: S M T W TH F S __/__/__

🏆 OVERALL TODAY WAS: ☆ ☆ ☆ ☆ ☆

😄 TODAY'S TRIUMPHS

_____
_____
_____
_____
_____
_____
_____
_____
_____
_____

🤔 TODAY'S CHALLENGES

_____
_____
_____
_____
_____
_____
_____
_____
_____
_____

💡 WHAT I LEARNED FROM TODAY:

_____

🏆 MY TOP GOAL FOR TOMORROW:

_____

DRAW ABOUT IT

DATE: S M T W TH F S __ / __ / __

🏆 OVERALL TODAY WAS: ☆ ☆ ☆ ☆ ☆

😄 TODAY'S TRIUMPHS

_____
_____
_____
_____
_____
_____
_____
_____
_____
_____

🤭 TODAY'S CHALLENGES

_____
_____
_____
_____
_____
_____
_____
_____
_____
_____

💡 WHAT I LEARNED FROM TODAY:

_____

🏆 MY TOP GOAL FOR TOMORROW:

_____

DRAW ABOUT IT

DATE: S M T W TH F S __ / __ / __

⊞ OVERALL TODAY WAS: ☆ ☆ ☆ ☆ ☆

😄 TODAY'S TRIUMPHS

_____
_____
_____
_____
_____
_____
_____
_____
_____
_____

😋 TODAY'S CHALLENGES

_____
_____
_____
_____
_____
_____
_____
_____
_____
_____

💡 WHAT I LEARNED FROM TODAY:

_____

🏆 MY TOP GOAL FOR TOMORROW:

_____

DRAW ABOUT IT

DATE: S M T W TH F S __/__/__

🏆 OVERALL TODAY WAS: ☆ ☆ ☆ ☆ ☆

😃 TODAY'S TRIUMPHS

_____
_____
_____
_____
_____
_____
_____
_____
_____
_____

😋 TODAY'S CHALLENGES

_____
_____
_____
_____
_____
_____
_____
_____
_____
_____

💡 WHAT I LEARNED FROM TODAY:

_____

🏆 MY TOP GOAL FOR TOMORROW:

_____

DRAW ABOUT IT

DATE: S M T W TH F S __ / __ / __

OVERALL TODAY WAS: ☆ ☆ ☆ ☆ ☆

😄 TODAY'S TRIUMPHS

_____
_____
_____
_____
_____
_____
_____
_____
_____

🤤 TODAY'S CHALLENGES

_____
_____
_____
_____
_____
_____
_____
_____
_____
_____

💡 WHAT I LEARNED FROM TODAY:

_____

🏆 MY TOP GOAL FOR TOMORROW:

_____

DRAW ABOUT IT

DATE: S M T W TH F S __ / __ / __

⬚ OVERALL TODAY WAS: ☆ ☆ ☆ ☆ ☆

☺ TODAY'S TRIUMPHS

_____
_____
_____
_____
_____
_____
_____
_____
_____
_____

☺ TODAY'S CHALLENGES

_____
_____
_____
_____
_____
_____
_____
_____
_____
_____

💡 WHAT I LEARNED FROM TODAY:

_____

🏆 MY TOP GOAL FOR TOMORROW:

_____

DRAW ABOUT IT

DATE: S M T W TH F S __/__/__

📊 OVERALL TODAY WAS: ☆ ☆ ☆ ☆ ☆

😄 TODAY'S TRIUMPHS

_____
_____
_____
_____
_____
_____
_____
_____
_____
_____

🤭 TODAY'S CHALLENGES

_____
_____
_____
_____
_____
_____
_____
_____
_____
_____

💡 WHAT I LEARNED FROM TODAY:

_____

🏆 MY TOP GOAL FOR TOMORROW:

_____

DRAW ABOUT IT

DATE: S M T W TH F S __ / __ / __

OVERALL TODAY WAS: ☆ ☆ ☆ ☆ ☆

😄 TODAY'S TRIUMPHS

_____
_____
_____
_____
_____
_____
_____
_____
_____
_____

😋 TODAY'S CHALLENGES

_____
_____
_____
_____
_____
_____
_____
_____
_____
_____

💡 WHAT I LEARNED FROM TODAY:

_____

🏆 MY TOP GOAL FOR TOMORROW:

_____

DRAW ABOUT IT

DATE: S M T W TH F S __ / __ / __

🏆 OVERALL TODAY WAS: ☆ ☆ ☆ ☆ ☆

😄 TODAY'S TRIUMPHS

_____
_____
_____
_____
_____
_____
_____
_____
_____

😋 TODAY'S CHALLENGES

_____
_____
_____
_____
_____
_____
_____
_____
_____

💡 WHAT I LEARNED FROM TODAY:

_____

🏆 MY TOP GOAL FOR TOMORROW:

_____

DRAW ABOUT IT

DATE: S M T W TH F S __ / __ / __

🏆 OVERALL TODAY WAS: ☆ ☆ ☆ ☆ ☆

😄 TODAY'S TRIUMPHS

_____
_____
_____
_____
_____
_____
_____
_____
_____
_____
_____

🤔 TODAY'S CHALLENGES

_____
_____
_____
_____
_____
_____
_____
_____
_____
_____
_____

💡 WHAT I LEARNED FROM TODAY:

_____

🏆 MY TOP GOAL FOR TOMORROW:

_____

DRAW ABOUT IT

DATE: S M T W TH F S ___ / ___ /___

🏆 OVERALL TODAY WAS: ☆ ☆ ☆ ☆ ☆

😄 TODAY'S TRIUMPHS

_____
_____
_____
_____
_____
_____
_____
_____
_____
_____

😋 TODAY'S CHALLENGES

_____
_____
_____
_____
_____
_____
_____
_____
_____
_____

💡 WHAT I LEARNED FROM TODAY:

_____

🏆 MY TOP GOAL FOR TOMORROW:

_____

DRAW ABOUT IT

DATE: S M T W TH F S __ / __ / __

OVERALL TODAY WAS: ☆ ☆ ☆ ☆ ☆

☺ TODAY'S TRIUMPHS

_____
_____
_____
_____
_____
_____
_____
_____
_____
_____

😋 TODAY'S CHALLENGES

_____
_____
_____
_____
_____
_____
_____
_____
_____
_____

💡 WHAT I LEARNED FROM TODAY:

_____

🏆 MY TOP GOAL FOR TOMORROW:

_____

DRAW ABOUT IT

DATE: S M T W TH F S __ / __ / __

🏆 OVERALL TODAY WAS: ☆ ☆ ☆ ☆ ☆

😄 TODAY'S TRIUMPHS

_____
_____
_____
_____
_____
_____
_____
_____
_____
_____

🤔 TODAY'S CHALLENGES

_____
_____
_____
_____
_____
_____
_____
_____
_____
_____

💡 WHAT I LEARNED FROM TODAY:

_____

🏆 MY TOP GOAL FOR TOMORROW:

_____

DRAW ABOUT IT